Contents

The mind-blowing music business

The music business is exciting! There are talented musicians, awesome albums and mind-blowing concerts. But you won't hear all the music news on the radio.

Take a look at some little-known facts about the music industry. Do you know which singer worked as an Elvis **impersonator** before he started school? Who performed a show in a school canteen? Which of your favourite singers don't use their real names? And what are their real names? Get ready to rethink what you know about the world of music.

EDGE BOOKS

Not Your Ordinary Trivia

MUSIC TRIVIA

What You Never Knew About Rock Stars, Recording Studios and Smash-Hit Songs

Raintree is an imprint of Capstone Global Library Limited, a company incorporated in England and Wales having its registered office at 264 Banbury Road, Oxford, OX2 7DY – Registered company number: 6695582

www.raintree.co.uk
myorders@raintree.co.uk

Edited by Mandy Robbins
Designed by Juliette Peters
Picture research by Jo Miller
Production by Tori Abraham
Originated by Capstone Global Library Ltd
Printed and bound in India

ISBN 978 1 4747 5945 8
22 21 20 19 18
10 9 8 7 6 5 4 3 2 1

British Library Cataloguing in Publication Data
A full catalogue record for this book is available from the British Library.

Acknowledgements
We would like to thank the following for permission to reproduce photographs: Getty Images: Catherine McGann/Contributor, 12t, Dave J Hogan/Contributor, 20t, Jesse Grant/Contributor, 26t, KMazur/ Contributor, 15t, Michael Tran/Contributor, 10t, Theo Wargo/Staff, 25; Newscom: MAVRIXONLINE.COM, 9, MEGA/Palace Lee, 11b, PacificCoastNews, 28t, 29b, Reuters/Mario Anzuoni, 8l, Reuters/Mike Blake, 23b, Splash News, 22b, Splash/Whittle, 7t, WENN/Carsten Windhorst, 13t; Shutterstock: A.PAES, 26br, Andy Dean Photography, 24t, Anna Kucherova, 18t, aragami12345s, 8r, ben bryant, 17b, camilkuo, 21m, Christian Bertrand, 21b, Csanad Kiss, 27t, dwphotos, 22t, 30-31, 32, Elena Butinova, 26bl, Es75, 19b, ESB Professional, 14br, Everett Collection, 7b, everydoghasastory, 29t, Evikka, 10b, FeatureFlash Photo Agency, 14bl, 27b, Ferdiperdozniy, 19m, Goran Djukanovic, 4-5, HikoPhotography, 19tr, igorstevanovic, 15b, Janis Smits, 28b, JStone, 18b, kamnuan, 27bl, Kathy Hutchins, 19tl, 24b, Ksenia Palimski, 11t, Macrovector, 16b, Marcin Kadziolka, 6, mariakraynova, 21t, Muellek Josef, 20b, OSABEE, 16t, PetlinDmitry, 27br, Photo Melon, 9l, sababa66, 1, Smileus, 12b, Tinseltown, 17t, Who is Danny, 13b, wideonet, 15m, yakub88, 14t, zcw, 9r, Zoa-Arts, cover
Design elements: Shutterstock: KannaA, Pakpoom Phummee, Zoa-Arts

impersonator someone who pretends to be someone else

CHAPTER 1

Home sweet home

Many famous musicians worked hard to become successful. Maybe they played on the street for coins. Maybe they performed in run-down clubs for little pay. What happened when these stars made it? They splurged on amazing homes.

Drake's LA mansion is full of things to do. He has indoor games such as table tennis, table football, pool, pinball and air hockey games. Do you like to read? Drake has a library full of books. His swimming pool even has waterfalls and a built-in stone cave!

Have you ever been at a party and had to wait in a queue for the toilets? That probably wouldn't happen at rapper 50 Cent's house in Connecticut. It has 35 bathrooms! With 19 bedrooms, there's plenty of space for visitors too.

chalet wooden house with a sloping roof

Justin Timberlake can practically tour the United States by visiting his own homes. He has a mansion in Hollywood Hills, California. He owns a country estate near Nashville, Tennessee. His ski **chalet** is near Big Sky, Montana. He also owns two expensive homes in New York City.

Justin Timberlake's home in Hollywood Hills, California

In 2017, Jay-Z and Beyoncé became the owners of one of the most expensive houses ever sold in Los Angeles County. Their property cost $90 million! It has six different buildings including staff housing. Bulletproof windows offer security to the couple. And if they want to go for a dip, there are four swimming pools to choose from.

CHAPTER 2

Tattoos, hairstyles and wild fashion choices

Many famous musicians have fun with fashion, hairstyles and tattoos. Some stick to a **signature** look. Others keep fans guessing.

Lady Gaga wore a dress made out of raw meat to the 2010 MTV Video Music Awards. It weighed about 23 kilograms (50 pounds). Gaga told reporters the dress was a statement to encourage people to stand up for their beliefs.

Bjork is a singer from Iceland. She is known for her bold, unique fashion choices. She once attended the Oscars dressed as a swan. Her dress was made of swan and goose feathers, felt and suede. It even had a head! Bjork scattered ostrich eggs on the red carpet. One thing was certain – her outfit ruffled fashion writers' feathers!

Nicki Minaj is known for the rainbow of hair colours she's had. But her jewellery choices might make fans hungry. The funky pop diva has worn food-themed necklaces. One looked like pink fried chicken. Another was a giant ice cream cone. She once wore a lilac pretzel too!

signature distinctive mark or characteristic associated with an individual

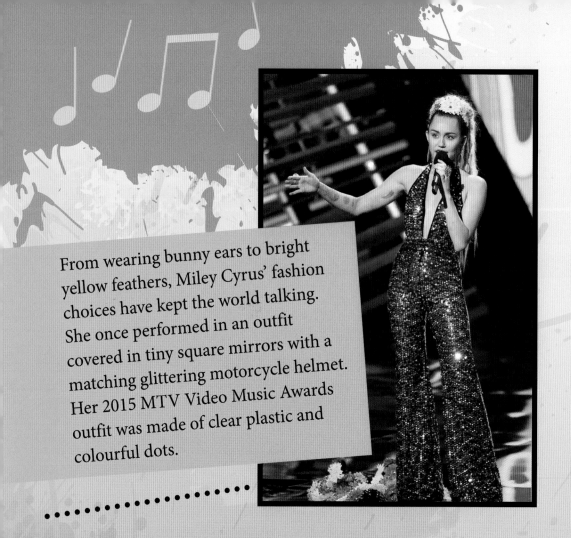

From wearing bunny ears to bright yellow feathers, Miley Cyrus' fashion choices have kept the world talking. She once performed in an outfit covered in tiny square mirrors with a matching glittering motorcycle helmet. Her 2015 MTV Video Music Awards outfit was made of clear plastic and colourful dots.

Ke$ha arrived at the 2010 MTV Video Music Awards wearing a dress made out of bin bags. The artist made the dress herself. What goes with shiny black plastic? Ke$ha paired the slick dress with a fur collar. And she wore her hair in a waist-length blonde plait.

In 2012, Rihanna got a large tattoo on her chest. It shows the ancient Egyptian goddess Isis. She represents the eternal mother and the goddess of fertility. The tattoo was Rihanna's tribute to her grandmother, Dolly, who had recently died.

Many music stars are covered in tattoos. Taylor Swift stands out because she doesn't have any. And she is pretty sure she'd never get a tattoo. Why not? Taylor doesn't think she could choose one symbol or saying for the rest of her life. She does sometimes write song lyrics on her arm, but they wash off.

CHAPTER 3

Before they were famous

Few musicians are born famous. Many had other jobs before they were famous. Find out what some of your favourite artists used to do.

Bruno Mars is from Hawaii. At the age of four, he worked as a mini Elvis impersonator. At the age of six, he appeared as little Elvis in the film *Honeymoon in Vegas*. Mars was credited as Bruno Hernandez in the film credits. But his real name is actually Peter Gene Hernandez.

Rock star legend Jon Bon Jovi had the Christmas spirit before becoming successful in the 1980s. Long before recording a song for the album *ICON Edition: A Very Special Christmas*, he had a job making Christmas decorations.

The rapper Example had a pretty cool job before making it in the music business. Example's real name is Elliot Gleave. He worked in the props department on the film *Star Wars Episode III: Revenge of the Sith*.

Before becoming a successful rapper, Macklemore worked in a prison for young offenders. As part of this job, he ran writing workshops. He also worked as a security guard in a prison. He once told an interviewer, "I definitely broke up fights."

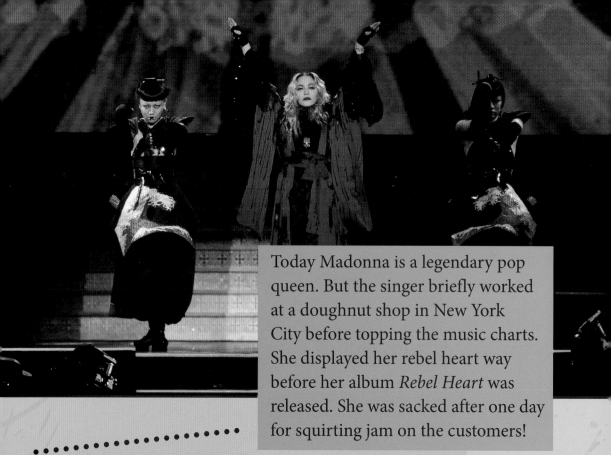

Today Madonna is a legendary pop queen. But the singer briefly worked at a doughnut shop in New York City before topping the music charts. She displayed her rebel heart way before her album *Rebel Heart* was released. She was sacked after one day for squirting jam on the customers!

Before becoming a rock star, Jack White was skilled at covering furniture. He owned a business called Third Man **Upholstery**. Jack would drive around Detroit looking for old furniture to reupholster.

upholstery stuffing, cushions and coverings that are put on furniture

What did Kurt Cobain do before becoming a rock legend in the early 1990s? The Nirvana **frontman** worked as a caretaker at a high school. Maybe cleaning out the locker rooms inspired him to write his hit song, "Smells Like Teen Spirit".

frontman leader of a music group; usually the lead singer

Before Beyoncé had her own team of hair stylists, she worked at her mother's hairdressers in Houston, Texas. Here "Queen Bey" earned money sweeping up hair. What did she do when she wasn't sweeping? She sang her heart out to the customers!

Hip-hop superstar J. Cole had an interesting job as a teenager. He worked at a local roller skating rink in Fayetteville, North Carolina. Part of his job was dressing up as a kangaroo to entertain customers!

CHAPTER 4

In the recording studio

Rock stars dream of making awesome music and selling millions of albums around the world. But no two artists record their music in exactly the same way. Find out more about what happens when artists are creating their musical masterpieces!

The Red Hot Chili Peppers recorded an album in a house that was said to be haunted. The previous owner was the legendary magician Harry Houdini!

Jay-Z's process of song creation doesn't involve pens or paper. First he listens to the music. Then he steps into a recording booth and starts saying lyrics as they come to him.

Kanye West recorded his hit single "Through the Wire" after a near-fatal car accident. West's jaw was wired shut while he was recording the song. That's how the song got its title.

Singing in the shower makes everyone's voice sound better. In his early days, Drake used a bath as a vocal booth to record some of his music. He sings about this experience in the hit song "Where Ya At".

CHAPTER 5

Life on the road

Being on the road can be fun for music stars. It can also be stressful. Some musicians are very particular about their hotel rooms and backstage areas. Here are some interesting preferences and habits performers have when on the road.

Jennifer Lopez is known for her long list of demands when travelling. She has very specific requests for her dressing room. The room must be white. It must have a white table, white flowers, a white sofa and white candles. And the drinking water must be at room temperature.

On her "Stars Dance" tour, Selena Gomez often had incense burning backstage when hanging out with her dancers. She also brought bikes and scooters to ride around on to keep the vibe fun and active.

Even pop stars have their food preferences. Ed Sheeran requests a few cans of fizzy drink and manuka honey from New Zealand. Rihanna asks for Cheetos, coconut water, Oreos, garlic olives and several more speciality items.

manuka honey

As part of his "We Don't Talk" tour, fans could buy a VIP upgrade called "Tea and Cookies with Charlie Puth". In addition to a backstage tour, these lucky fans could enjoy some of Puth's favourite foods while hanging out with the celebrity.

For her 777 tour, Rihanna played seven concerts in seven different countries in seven days. In Europe she rocked out in France, Sweden, Germany and the UK. In North America she jammed in Mexico, Canada and the United States.

On their flight to Atlanta, Georgia, Imagine Dragons played live, without drums, at 9,144 metres (30,000 feet). They used the flight attendant's announcement speakerphone to increase the volume of their own small **amplifiers**.

amplifier piece of equipment that makes sound louder

Concerts aren't always on dry land. Some musicians play on cruise ships. The band Paramour called their cruise-ship performance "Parahoy!".

Hold your nose! The **ska**-punk group The King Blues played three shows in the sewer system below Brighton Pier. These gigs were part of a UK music festival that had shows in unusual locations such as churches, museums and markets.

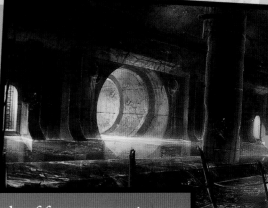

ska style of fast pop music with Jamaican roots

Do you ever wish something cool would happen at your school? Canadian band Arcade Fire played a show in the canteen at Canterbury High School in Ottawa, Ontario. Richard Reed Parry, one of the band members, had gone to school there.

21

Irish rock band U2 is no stranger to touring. Their 360° Tour was both the highest-**grossing** and the most-attended tour in history. More than 7.2 million people came to the 110 shows. The band sold more than $736 million worth of tickets!

grossing money earned before taxes are removed

Stars love to play at New York's legendary Madison Square Garden. But fans have to be quick to get a ticket for some artists. Justin Bieber sold out two shows there in just 30 seconds! Each show offered 20,000 seats.

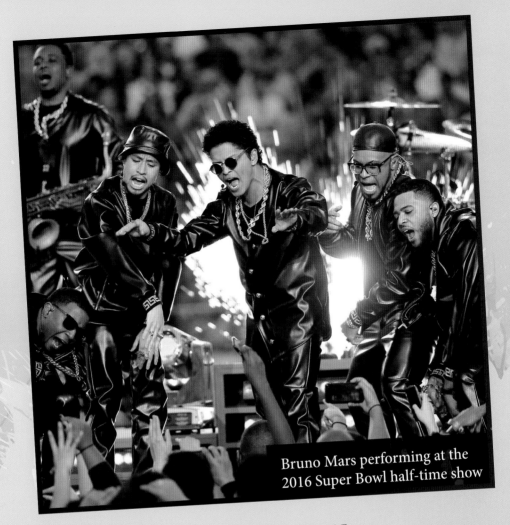

Bruno Mars performing at the
2016 Super Bowl half-time show

The performance may last less than 15 minutes, but some of the biggest artists in history have rocked the NFL Super Bowl half-time show. Bruno Mars, Madonna and Prince are among them. The most-viewed Super Bowl half-time performance was by Lady Gaga in 2017. About 118 million people watched it live, and more than 150 million more viewed it online afterwards.

When rock stars go on tour, many fly on a private jet. But Taylor Swift doesn't just have her own plane. She has her own airport **hangar** at the Nashville International Airport.

hangar large building where planes are kept

The super rich can hire popular musicians to play for private events. But the price is steep! Kanye West earned a cool $3 million playing at a wedding for the grandson of the President of Kazakhstan. Christina Aguilera once charged $3.6 million to sing three songs at the wedding of a Russian billionaire. That's more than $1 million per song! Do you want a bargain? Usher will sing "Happy Birthday" at an event for just $250,000.

Rock stars have played their music all around the world. But many of the biggest names in music have appeared on *Sesame Street*. Train, Bruno Mars, Usher, Queen Latifah, Alicia Keys, LL Cool J and Will.i.am are some of them. Queen Latifah rapped about the letter O. Alicia Keys mimicked her song "Fallin'" by singing one called "Dancin" with Elmo. LL Cool J went on an "Addition Expedition".

CHAPTER 6

Pampered pets

Many music stars are animal lovers. But their pets can be more pampered than most. They often live a rock star lifestyle, too. Some pets even inspire new songs.

A number of stars have named their pets after other famous artists. Kelly Clarkson named her goat after singer Billy Joel. Pink once had a bulldog called Elvis. Nick Jonas also honoured his favourite artist by calling his dog Elvis.

Katy Perry is a huge cat fan. She named her cat Kitty Purry. This famous cat was **nominated** for a Teen Choice Award for Best Celebrity Pet.

nominate name someone as a candidate for an award or job

Rick Springfield was a 1980s pop star. He found his dog homeless in a California car park. The singer named the dog Lethal Ron for a funny reason. According to Rick, the dog had horribly bad gas. Lethal Ron appeared on two of Springfield's album covers. They were called *Working Class Dog* and *Success Hasn't Spoiled Me Yet.*

Some stars choose unusual pets. Justin Bieber once owned a pet capuchin monkey called Mally. Miley Cyrus has a pet pig named Pig Pig. And Willow Smith has several snakes as pets. She even lets them curl up in bed with her!

Miley Cyrus was devastated when her dog Floyd died. She sang to a giant blow-up statue of him as part of her Bangerz tour. She also sang a cover of the Coldplay song "The Scientist" and dedicated it to Floyd.

The band Japanese Breakfast's song "In Heaven" refers to singer Michelle Zauner's dog, Julia. The song describes Julia's reaction to the death of Michelle's mum, who had been the main person to look after the dog.

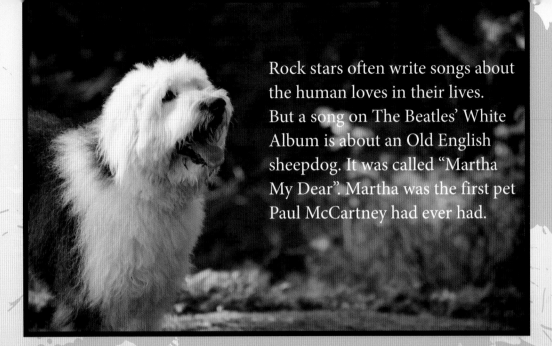

Rock stars often write songs about the human loves in their lives. But a song on The Beatles' White Album is about an Old English sheepdog. It was called "Martha My Dear". Martha was the first pet Paul McCartney had ever had.

In 2015, John Legend filmed a wedding between his dogs Puddy and Pippa. The dogs were dressed in traditional wedding clothing. Legend sang his song "All of Me" to them.

The music industry can be creative, exciting and surprising. Musicians love to push boundaries and entertain fans. You never know what might happen in the world of music!

Glossary

amplifier piece of equipment that makes sound louder

chalet wooden house with a sloping roof

frontman leader of a music group; usually the lead singer

grossing money earned before taxes are removed

hangar large building where planes are kept

impersonator someone who pretends to be someone else

nominate name someone as a candidate for an award or job

signature distinctive mark or characteristic associated with an individual

ska style of fast pop music with Jamaican roots

upholstery stuffing, cushions and coverings that are put on furniture

Find out more

Books

Children's Book of Music, DK (DK Children, 2010)

Create Your Own Music (Media Genius), Matthew Anniss (Raintree, 2017)

The Impact of Technology in Music (The Impact of Technology), Matthew Anniss (Raintree, 2016)

Jay-Z (Titans of Business), Richard Spilsbury (Raintree, 2013)

Website

www.dkfindout.com/uk/music-art-and-literature/types-music
Find out more about different types of music from around the world.

Index